SOLVE IT
⇌ WITH ⇌
SHERLOCK HOLMES

WELBECK

Published in 2019 by Welbeck Children's
An Imprint of Welbeck Children's Limited,
part of the Welbeck Publishing Group
Offices in: London - 20 Mortimer Street, London W1T 3JW &
Sydney - Level 17, 207 Kent St, Sydney NSW 2000 Australia
www.welbeckpublishing.com

A catalogue record for this book is available from the British Library.

ISBN 978-1-78312-402-2

Printed in China

Excecutive Editor: Bryony Davies
Design Manager: Emily Clarke
Designed by: Kate Wiliwinska
Production: Nicola Davey

SOLVE IT
⇉ WITH ⇇
SHERLOCK HOLMES

Written by
Gareth Moore

Illustrated by
Margarida Esteves

WELBECK

Welcome to Sherlock's Office

The world-famous detective Sherlock Holmes is the eccentric hero of a collection of stories written by Sir Arthur Conan Doyle. In case you are not familiar with him, let us introduce you: Holmes is a consulting detective, who lives at 221B Baker Street, London, with his partner, Dr John Watson.

Holmes uses his exceptional powers of observation, deduction and logical reasoning to solve mysteries, even those which baffle the police.

This puzzle book gives you exclusive access to Sherlock's office and private documents. You will encounter never-seen-before puzzles that Sherlock and Watson were called upon to solve in the course of their many adventures. Gathered within this book are almost 40 brainteasers that Holmes and Watson faced.

Can you use your own detective skills to help solve them all?

1. The Coded Tip

A strange note has been sent to Sherlock Holmes. He thinks it may be a tip-off regarding a criminal gang he's been following. A code has been applied to conceal the message, but luckily, Holmes has managed to work it out.

"Can you see what the message says?" Holmes asks his colleague, Dr Watson. "My informant has simply changed each letter of the alphabet to the one immediately before it. So, for example, he has changed B to A, C to B, and so on."

What does the message say?

UIF SPCCFSZ
XJMM CF BU
OPPO UPNPSSPX

2. Science Suspects

A famous scientist has been kidnapped. When Holmes and Watson arrive at his laboratory, they soon establish that the most likely suspects are his three colleagues: Michael, Harry and Tina.

However, the difficulty is in deciding which is the guilty one. After searching for a while they find an important clue: a note on the desk that appears to have been hurriedly written in the victim's handwriting.

The note seems to be revealing a scientific result:

It was titanium and sodium...

Can you examine the laboratory and work out who kidnapped the scientist?

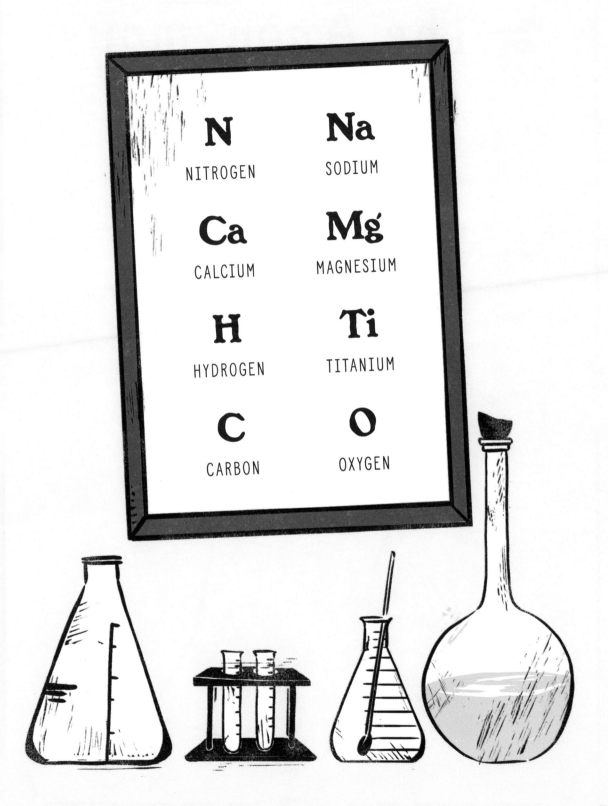

3. The Anonymous Letter

Mrs Jones is the owner of a large art gallery in London, not far from Holmes's offices in Baker Street. She has come to Holmes for help because she has received a strange letter, unsigned and in code, and wants to know what it says.

The letter consists of a sequence of pictures and symbols, as shown on the opposite page.

Holmes has seen this kind of message before. Using Holmes's notes on what various symbols are likely to mean, can you work out what the message says?

↺	It	⊙	Who
◀	You	✳	Be
→	Robbery	◆	Staff
↕	One	✳	A
∧	Is	▣	Your
◄	At	◈	Will
☾	Careful	⊗	Of
📄	Trust	▲	There
✕	Time	◇	Gallery

To Mrs J

✳ ☾

▲ ◈ ✳ ✳ → ◄ ▣ ◇

4. The Diamond Box

Holmes and Watson are searching a house for some stolen diamonds when they come across a box that has been locked with a three-digit combination code.

Luckily, the person who left the box has also left a note which gives clues to the code. Can you crack the three-digit code using just the following notes?

4 8 3 – One digit is correct but is on the wrong dial.

3 8 2 – One digit is correct and is on the correct dial.

1 8 3 – None of the digits are correct.

5 1 2 – Two digits are correct and are both on the correct dial.

5. Missing Keys

Mrs Hudson, Holmes's housekeeper, has muddled up the keys to the various rooms in 221B Baker Street.

Can you help her sort out the keys again by pairing each key with its correct lock silhouette?

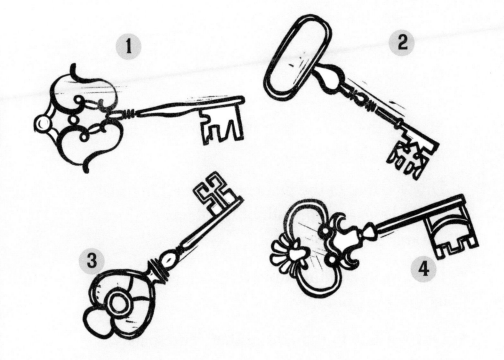

6. Moriarty's Warehouse

Holmes has happened upon a map that he believes will lead him to the house where the criminal mastermind, Professor James Moriarty, is storing all his stolen goods. If he can locate it, he may even find Moriarty too. He suspects it is on a particular street, but he does not yet know which house it is.

Can you follow the instructions to trace out a path that reveals the number of Moriarty's house?

- ◆ Start at the place which has a *face* and hands but not a single leg.

- ◆ Draw a line to the picture of something that could be used with both of the items in the squares directly beneath it.

- ◆ Draw a line to the thing that can contain letters, but isn't a book.

- ◆ Draw a line to something that represents the entire world.

- ◆ Draw a line to the object which has *fingers* but no toes.

- ◆ Draw a line to the item which represents what you're reading right now.

7. A Question of Rooms

Holmes and Watson are interviewing a witness to a theft that took place in a school. The witness has a hazy memory and only remembers a few facts about which room it took place in:

◆ It was not in a room that shares an entrance with the music room.

◆ The room had more than one entrance.

◆ The room was not next to the office.

◆ It did not happen in a room which connects to the auditorium.

Using the map of the school, can you work out what room the witness saw the theft take place in?

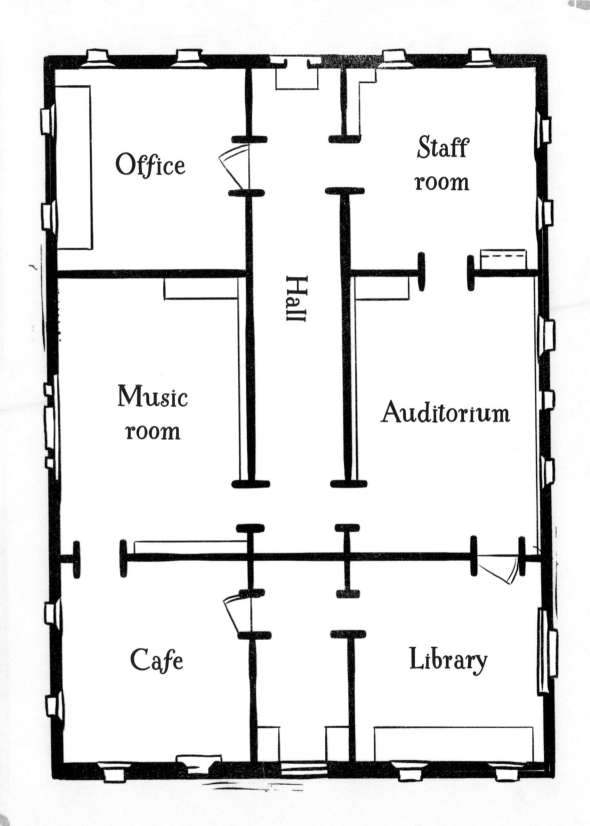

Office

Staff room

Hall

Music room

Auditorium

Cafe

Library

8. Holmes's Diary

Holmes is a very private man. All of the information in his diary is written in different types of code, to make it difficult for someone else to understand it. He even conceals important dates, to reduce the chance of a criminal intercepting him on his travels.

Using the page from Holmes's diary below, can you work out the date of Watson's birth? Holmes has encoded the year, month and day separately, using three different mathematical sequences.

Watson's birth

7	10	16	25	37		Year
192	96	48	24	12		Month
41	40	37	32	25		Day

9. A Note from Holmes

Watson arrives home one afternoon and finds a note which Holmes has left for him. The note says:

"Watson, meet me at ▲ ■ ● Edgware Road."

As a clue, Holmes has also left the following additional information, scribbled further down the note:

● - 3 = 5   ■ + 2 = ●   ■ + ▲ = 9

Using these clues, at what house number on Edgware Road should Watson meet Holmes?

10. The Calendar Deduction

One of the police's case files, which contains important information about an unsolved crime, has gone missing. Holmes and Watson are interviewing the police detectives who compiled the original file in order to try and start a new file.

They are trying to work out on what date the original crime took place. Between all of the detectives, this is what they remember:

- The crime took place in September.

- It did not take place on a day with a letter T in its name, such as Tuesday.

- The day of the month was not even.

- No other event was marked on the calendar for that day.

- It took place before the Escaped Horse Confusion.

- The day of the month was a two-digit number.

- No previous event had taken place on that same day earlier in the month.

On what date did the crime take place?

SEPTEMBER

SUN	MON	TUE	WED	THURS	FRI	SAT
	1	2	3	4 Museum Heist	5	6
7	8	9	10	11	12 Moriarty Mystery	13
14	15 Diamond Disaster	16	17 Parade Day	18	19	20
21	22	23	24	25 Savoy Theatre Crime	26	27
28 Escaped Horse Confusion	29	30 Leaving Gathering	31			

11. Identity Parade

Holmes and Watson are helping Inspector Lestrade, a detective at Scotland Yard, to investigate a burglary. Five suspects have been brought to Scotland Yard for an identity parade. They are all lined up along a wall, waiting for Mrs Smith to come in and try to identify the burglar she saw climbing out of her neighbour's front window.

Unfortunately, the detective's notes as to each person's name have become muddled up. Can you help assign the correct name to each person?

- ◆ Arthur is standing next to Thomas.
- ◆ Sebastian is standing on one of the two ends of the line.
- ◆ Jim is not standing next to Robert.
- ◆ Thomas is taller than Sebastian.
- ◆ Neither Arthur nor Jim are standing at either end of the line.

Which suspect is which?

12. A Criminal Pursuit

Pursuing a criminal can be hard work! Holmes has chased down a jewel thief who has led him into a warehouse full of strange corridors and passages.

Can you help Holmes find a route through the building, from top to bottom, so he can catch the thief before he escapes?

13. A Note for Watson

Watson often arrives home to find cryptic notes addressed to him laid out on the kitchen table. Ever the detective, Holmes can never write a simple note or ask a straightforward question without adding a brainteaser. One particular note has information regarding a party that Holmes and Watson have been invited to. It says:

> Watson,
>
> I have information about the day of the party. It is two days before the day that is three days after Wednesday.
>
> See you there, old chap!

What day is the party? Use the grid below to help you work it out.

Mon	Tue	Wed	Thurs	Fri	Sat	Sun

14. Holmes's Dominoes

Idleness is a sin according to Holmes. He likes to be busy and to keep his mind active. After all, he wouldn't be the world's greatest detective if he wasn't so sharp.

Holmes recently taught Watson a simple variation of the game of dominoes, in which the aim is to create a loop of touching dominoes.

In this game, as in any game of dominoes, the dominoes may only touch one another if they have the same number of spots on their two touching ends.

Can you place some of the leftover dominoes beneath into the gaps marked on the loop, in order to complete the game?

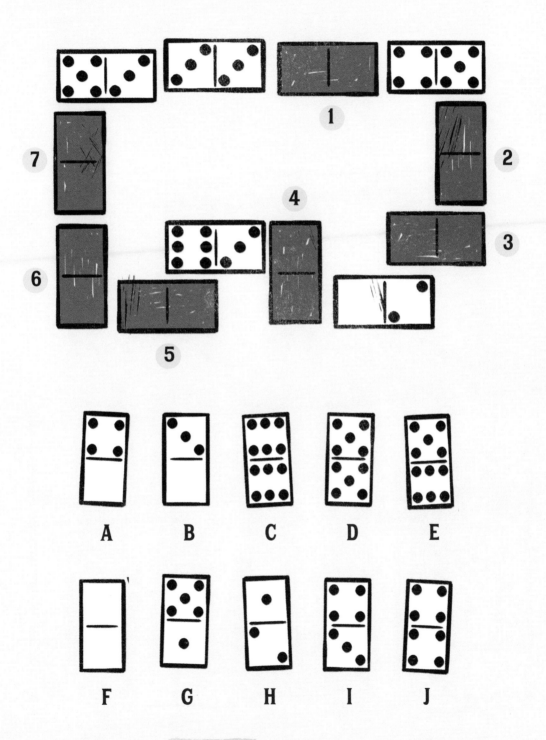

25

15. Mrs Hudson's Herbs

Mrs Hudson has bought five each of five different herbs, and wishes to plant them out in her herb garden. The herb garden is divided into five rows of five boxes, and she wants to place the herbs so that no two identical herbs are in touching boxes – not even diagonally. She also wants to make sure that there is only one of each herb planted in any individual row or column. She thinks that the garden will be most useful if arranged this way.

Some of the herbs have already been planted. Can you help Holmes plant the remainder of the herbs according to Mrs Hudson's wishes?

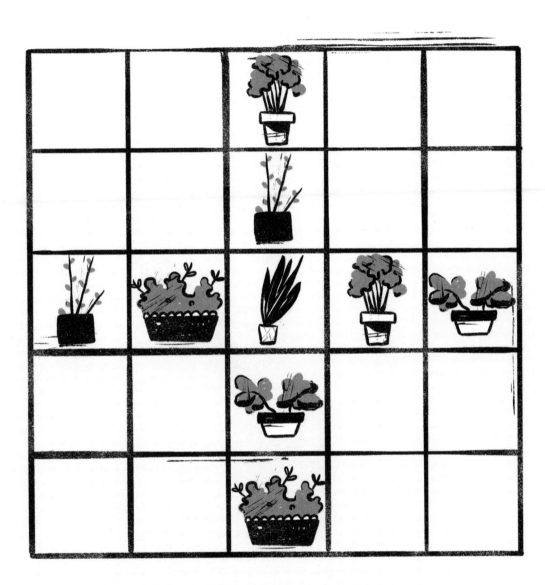

16. Travel Time

Holmes and Watson are travelling out of London to deal with a case in the countryside.

Holmes likes to plan carefully and wants to ensure that they arrive on time. He really dislikes being late.

Holmes works out that it will take them 30 minutes to walk to the train station. The train to their destination will then take them twice as long as the walk. Finally, the journey from the train station into the village will take a quarter of the length of the train journey.

How long will the journey take them?

17. The Case Files

Holmes was very busy last year, solving many cases. By reading the following clues, can you work out how many cases he solved in total?

+ In each of the last *four* months of the year, he solved the same number of crimes as the previous month.

+ In each month starting with an M, he solved the same number of cases.

+ There was one month in which he only solved two cases.

+ In each month starting with an A, he solved one more case than in the previous month, so for example in April he solved one more crime than in March.

+ In April he solved half of the number of cases he solved in July.

+ In each month starting with a J, he solved eight cases.

Month	No.	Month	No.	Month	No.

18. Moriarty's Map

"Well Watson, what do you make of this?" said Holmes to me over breakfast, casting a much-creased piece of paper onto the table.

I unfolded it and after close inspection, replied: "It appears to be a map."

"Not just any map," said Holmes excitedly. "This shows where Moriarty's gang will strike next. All we have to do is let Inspector Lestrade know where to catch the villains red-handed."

"But Holmes," I replied, looking again at the map, "there is clearly more than one place here that would be of interest to a gang of thieves."

Holmes smiled. "Look closely. The answer is in the code scribbled below the map."

Can you help Watson to work out where to catch Moriarty and his gang?

START

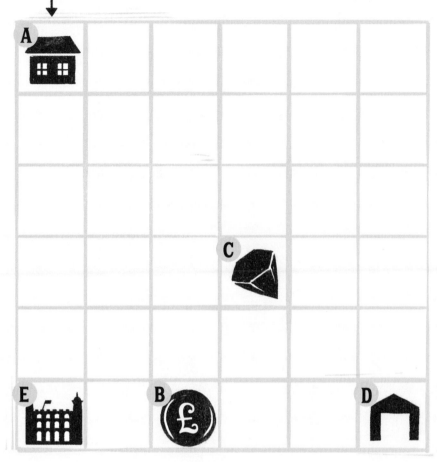

2↓ 4→ 2↓ 3← 1↓ 1←

KEY:

A: Professor Moriarty's house

B: The Bank of England

C: Clerkenwell diamond merchants

D: Isle of Dogs spice warehouse

E: Tower of London

19. The Innkeeper's Secret

Holmes and Watson recently travelled out of London to investigate a case. They always enjoy visiting somewhere new.

This particular case was located in Liverpool, where Holmes had come to question an innkeeper who was suspected of hiding stolen goods. Watson distracted him with a series of questions, while Holmes went to search his office. In the office, he found a hidden map, along with a set of instructions to use alongside the map. Holmes suspects that this map will lead them to the stolen goods.

Starting from the inn, can you use both the map on the opposite page and the clues below to help them find the stolen goods?

- ◆ Start at the inn.

- ◆ Move two blocks east.

- ◆ Move one block south.

- ◆ Move one block east.

- ◆ Move three blocks north.

- ◆ Move two blocks west.

- ◆ Move one block north.

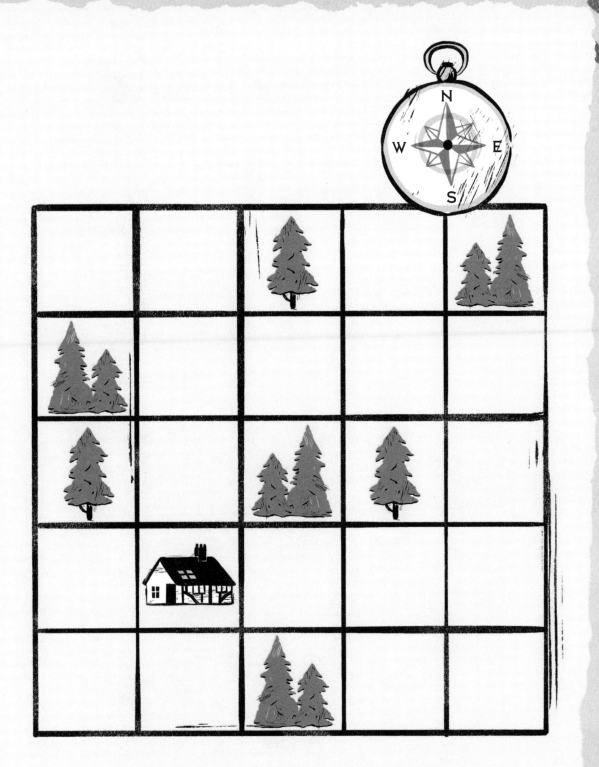

20. The Second Anonymous Letter

The gallery owner, Mrs Jones, has received a second anonymous letter. The letter is shown below.

Holmes has once again studied the code and written out some notes. By combining his notes here with those he made for Mrs Jones's first anonymous letter (see a previous case earlier in this book), can you decode this second hidden message?

⊠	Not	↺	Warning
▷	Yesterday	◢	Today
↰	Their	←	Them
➡	Do	➚	Your

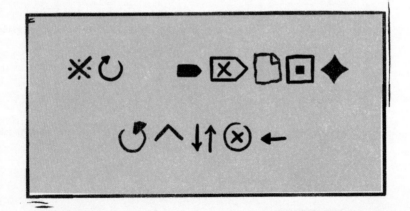

21. A Confusing Time

Holmes and Watson are trying to figure out the timings of a crime which took place yesterday at the London dockyards. In order to solve the case, they must figure out the working hours of each staff member.

Not everyone is as helpful as they could be. In particular, one person that Holmes is questioning today is being particularly indirect. When Holmes asks at what time they finished work at the dockyard on the day of the crime, they answer:

"It was 3 hours after the time which was as many hours after 7am as it was before 7pm."

What time are they referring to?

22. The Burglary Route

There is an informer in Moriarty's criminal gang. He sometimes gives Holmes and Watson important information about the gang's other members, and their plans for future crimes.

It is dangerous work for the informer because Moriarty would not be happy to discover that someone is giving away his secrets. For this reason, the informer never agrees to meet Holmes in person but will always send him letters instead. These letters are always coded in some way.

Yesterday, Holmes received a map which outlined the planned burglary route of the gang. They are to break into several houses along a specific route, ending up at a building Moriarty uses at the dockyard. The informer has sent directions from the start of their route but as Holmes doesn't know where they are starting from, he will need to follow them backwards from the dockyard, reversing every arrow.

Using the directions below and the map on the opposite page, can you work out which houses are on the burglary route?

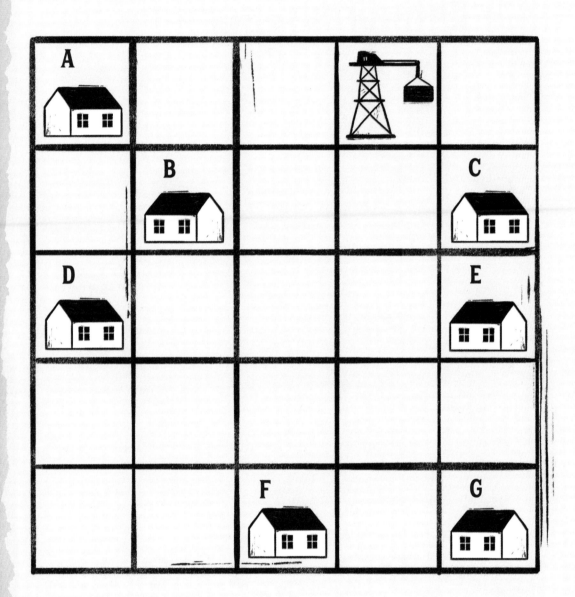

23. The Coffee House Suspects

Four possible suspects for a crime have been identified by an eyewitness. The crime took place at a coffee house in London, and each of the four suspects was seen visiting the coffee house at a different time that day.

Holmes has deduced that the crime took place at around 1:15pm. This means that to identify the correct suspect it is important that the eyewitness can remember when each of the suspects arrived at the coffee house.

This is what the eyewitness tells Holmes:

- None of the suspects stayed longer than half an hour.

- I saw each of them enter at a different time of day. One arrived at 10am, one at 11am, one at 1pm and one at 3pm.

- Suspect 1 arrived before Suspect 2.

- Suspect 2 arrived after Suspect 4 .

- Suspect 3 arrived first.

- Suspect 4 arrived after Suspect 1.

Can you work out at what time each suspect arrived, and therefore who is most likely to have committed the crime?

24. Library Logic

A member of Moriarty's gang has been pulled in for questioning. It is believed that he has hidden the plans for a bank robbery in a book in the public library.

The gang member is refusing to help, so Holmes has been called in to question him. Under Holmes's expert examination, the gang member does eventually reveal this piece of information:

> "The plan is in the book that is 4th from
> the left and 6th from the right."

Holmes realises that this allows him to work out how many books are on the shelf where the plan has been hidden. This will allow them to quickly find the correct shelf, and then the plan.

Can you work out how many books are on the shelf on which Holmes can find the robbery plans?

25. A Christmas Conundrum

Mrs Hudson has a huge family with many nieces and nephews. At Christmas time this means that she needs to buy a lot of gifts for all of them. Unfortunately, Mrs Hudson cannot remember the ages or hobbies of four of her nieces and nephews: Jean, Arthur, Mary and Lucas.

She does know that they each have one favourite hobby, and that these are painting, reading, swimming and playing guitar. She also knows that one of them is six years old, one is seven, one is nine and one is ten years old.

Mrs Hudson has asked Holmes to use his detective skills to help her figure out each child's age and their favourite hobby. This is the information she has given Holmes:

- ◆ Mary is younger than Lucas.
- ◆ The youngest child cannot read or swim.
- ◆ The seven-year-old likes playing the guitar.
- ◆ Arthur is two years younger than Mary.
- ◆ Lucas's hobby is swimming.

Using this information, can you help Holmes figure out the age and hobby of each child?

26. A Mystery Party

The Turners, who live across the road at 220 Baker Street, are hosting a party next week. The party will include a pretend crime, which will need to be solved by the guests.

The Turners have asked Holmes for his help to organise the party, and much against his will he has agreed. He has done this as a favour to Mrs Hudson, who is friends with the Turners.

Mr Turner wishes to divide the living room, using only straight lines of tape, into six separate sections. He wants to place the tape so that there are two pieces of evidence in each section, and he has provided Holmes with a plan of the living room so that he can prepare.

Currently the plan shows only the pieces of evidence. How can Holmes divide the room into six sections, using just three straight lines, so that there are exactly two pieces of evidence in each section?

27. The Hidden Suspect

A suspect for a robbery that took place at the train station has been identified, but unfortunately he has gone into hiding. The police have searched his usual hideaways, but have not been able to find him. His known associates are not giving anything away, either.

Recently, however, a strange map and some clues have been sent to Holmes by an informer. Holmes believes that the map may lead them to the thief's secret hiding place.

Here are the clues that arrived with the map:

- He is not hiding in a location that is in either the middle row or the middle column.

- He is not in a row that has a letter found in the word PUZZLE.

- He is not in any square in which the column number is equal to a letter at the same position in the alphabet, such as A1, B2, C3 and so on.

- He is in a row that comes later in the alphabet than A.

Can you use the clues to work out which house the suspect is hiding in?

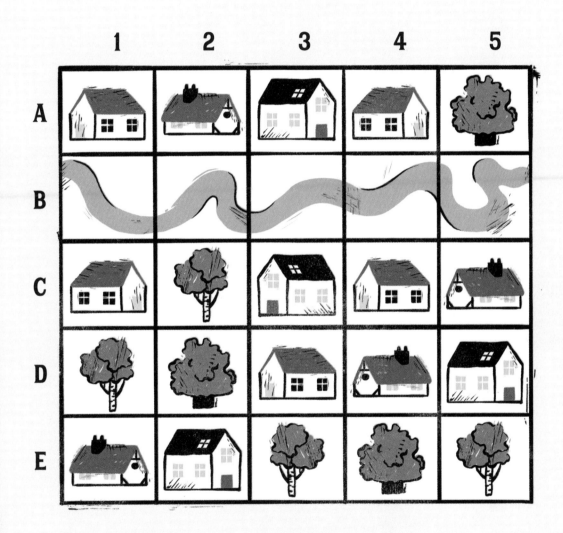

28. The Jewel Pouch

An arrest was made yesterday after a long investigation into the robbery of a very wealthy family's house. All of the jewels had been stolen out of their safe, and the family had been very anxious to recover them.

It was Holmes, of course, who solved the case. He had found some strands of blonde hair and a staff key that led to an expensive restaurant in London. After questioning the staff members at the restaurant, Holmes had searched through their lockers and found a small pouch of stolen jewels.

Holmes observed that all but two of the jewels were rubies, that all but two of them were emeralds, and that all but two of them were diamonds.

How many jewels did Holmes find in the pouch?

29. The Narrow Doorway

Holmes's detective work has led to the swift arrest of a thief that had been stealing from a street in which three members of Mrs Hudson's family lived. To celebrate the occasion, they invite Holmes and Watson to a nearby coffee house for a hot drink. Watson convinces Holmes that he should attend, but Holmes cannot help but make a puzzle out of the event.

Holmes notes first that there are five of them there: himself and Watson, plus Mrs Hudson's relatives who are named Mark, Nina and Ruth. Next he observes that they had each passed through the narrow doorway one by one, and he challenges them to remember the order they had entered. No one can recall the exact answer, so Holmes gives them these clues:

◆ Holmes entered directly behind Nina.

◆ Watson entered before Ruth did.

◆ Mark was neither the first nor the last to enter.

◆ Ruth was the third to enter.

Can you work out in which order they entered the coffee house?

30. The Number Clues

Watson is often left cryptic notes and clues by Holmes. Holmes does like to make a game out of what would ordinarily be a simple matter of writing down a date, address, name or what-have-you. Holmes claims that he does this because detectives should always practice their logic skills, but Watson is not sure if he believes this is his real reason.

Today, Mrs Hudson hands Watson a note that has been left for him by Holmes. The note says:

> We have an exciting case to attend to, my dear Watson. I need you to be sharp and alert because it is one that is sure to require you to pay attention!
>
> Please meet me at 5pm today at Marylebone Apartments. The number of the apartment is hidden in the puzzle attached.
>
> Just read across the missing numbers.
>
> See you there, old chap.
>
> S.H.

The note also includes the following sketches:

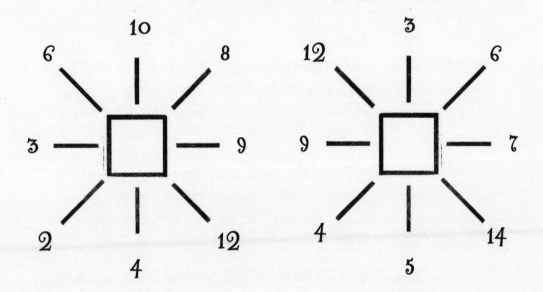

Watson has seen this type of puzzle before, and knows that he needs to write a number in each of the two boxes. Each number needs to be chosen so that it forms a mathematical sum along every line in the diagram. This would mean that you could take, for example, the 2 in the first picture, add on the number in the box, and then the result would be the 8 on the opposite side.

Can you write the correct number in each box in order to work out the apartment number?

31. On the Hunt

Two of Mrs Hudson's nieces are spending the weekend at Baker Street. Holmes normally entertains both himself and the children by telling them fantastical stories that contain hidden puzzles. However, this is a special weekend – it is Easter.

Holmes has decided to create an Easter-egg hunt where the children must find as many eggs as possible. However, Holmes being Holmes, he has hidden them far too well and after an hour they have failed to find any of them.

Watson proposes giving them some clues, so Holmes finally agrees to provide a map and some additional hints. In this way they can at least be sure to find some of the eggs.

Can you use the map opposite and the following directions to help the girls find some of the eggs? The squares on the grid represent steps in Holmes's living room. The edges of the map represent the walls, and none of the instructions require the children to walk into walls!

- You are *facing* west at the position marked with an X. Move one step *forward* (in the direction you are *facing*).

- Turn 90 degrees and move three steps *forward*.

- Turn 90 degrees and move one step *forward*.

- Turn to face north and move one step *forward*.

- Turn 90 degrees and move two steps *forward*.

- Turn 90 degrees and move three steps forward.

- Turn to face west and move one step forward.

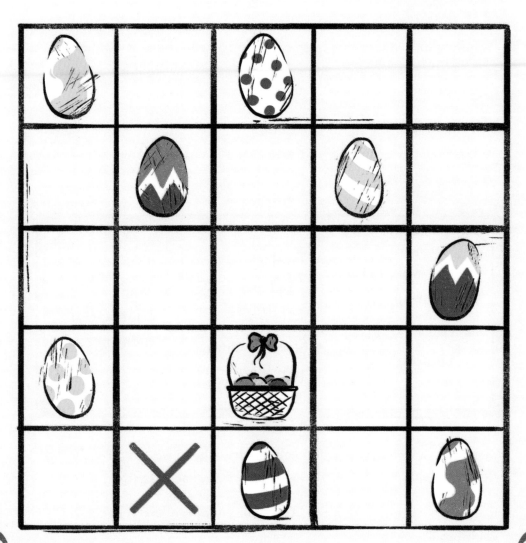

32. A Painting Problem

The Dulwich Picture Gallery in London has been robbed! The police claim it is the largest robbery that has ever taken place at an art gallery.

Holmes and Watson have been called in to head the investigation, in the hope of recovering the priceless works of art that have been stolen.

The gallery is trying to work out how many paintings have been taken. So far, they have counted how many are missing from the works of five well-known artists:

- Ten BOTTICELLI paintings
- Seven DA VINCI paintings
- Twelve MICHELANGELO paintings
- Seven RAPHAEL paintings
- Nine REMBRANDT paintings

Holmes quickly spots that the robbers have been working to a pattern that tells them how many works to steal from each artist.

Can you spot the pattern too? Can you say how many TITIAN paintings were stolen?

33. The Alibi Arrest

Three suspects are being questioned at Scotland Yard by Holmes. Two days ago, there was a massive thunderstorm and such heavy rain that all of the gas lights on the street were extinguished. This gave a certain burglar the opportunity to break into three houses on a single street!

Three suspects, all of whom fit the description given by an eyewitness, have been asked to provide an alibi to Holmes:

"I work as a caretaker, and that evening I had to work late," the first suspect tells Holmes.

"I was having an evening picnic in the park with my wife," the second suspect says.

"You can speak to my French tutor, who will tell you that I was busy learning French," the last suspect says.

Holmes is immediately sure that he knows which suspect is lying, and has him arrested. Who do you think he suspects?

34. A Test of Time

Holmes walks into the living room one day and is surprised to find Watson firmly tapping his pocket watch on the desk.

"My pocket watch had stopped working," Watson tells Holmes, "but I think I have managed to fix it. What is the current time, Holmes?"

Holmes knows that Watson simply wants to set his watch to the correct time, but he can't help but set him a brainteaser rather than give a direct answer. Holmes tells Watson:

"The number of hours left today is half of the number of hours that have already passed."

What time should Watson set his watch to?

35. The Dancing Duos

Last night, Holmes and Watson were accompanied by Mrs Hudson and Mrs Jones to the annual Scotland Yard Ball. It is a fancy event attended by the best detectives and officers in the country, which was the only reason that Holmes agreed to go.

Unfortunately, there is always a surge in criminal activity in the city on the night of the Ball. This is because most of London's best police officers are at the Ball instead of working!

Holmes, Watson, Mrs Hudson and Mrs Jones were seated at a table with people who, according to their place cards, were called Mr Bradley, Ms White, Mr Jake and Mrs Reece.

It was required that one of each of Holmes's group would partner with one person from the other group at the table, to dance.

- ◆ Each person partnered with a person of the opposite gender.

- ◆ Holmes did not waltz with Mrs Reece.

- ◆ Mrs Hudson's partner had a two-syllable surname.

- ◆ Mrs Jones found a partner with the same initials as her.

Can you figure out who partnered with whom?

36. A Quick Way Home

After tying up a case in Chippenham, Holmes and Watson are eager to get home. At the railway station they assess their options for the best way home:

- One train leaves in twenty minutes, takes one hour and will arrive at Paddington Station – which is a 10-minute walk from home.

- Another train leaves immediately, takes 1 hour and 10 minutes, and will arrive at Victoria Station – which is a 25-minute walk from home.

- The last train leaves in 15 minutes, takes 50 minutes and will arrive at Liverpool Street Station, which is a 35-minute walk from home.

Which train should they take if their aim is to arrive home as soon as possible?

37. The Four Criminals

Watson has discovered over many years that there are a large number of people in London who make a life out of crime. Usually the crimes are small, such as petty theft. The thieves are sometimes caught and locked up, but the jails are so crowded that they are often released before long to continue their lives of small-time crime.

In the holding cells of Scotland Yard, there are currently four such petty criminals: Jo, Lena, Archie and Duke. They are bragging to one another about the number of thefts they have committed this year.

Holmes overhears their conversation, and this is what he learns from it:

- One of them committed 16 crimes, one committed 19 crimes, one committed 23 crimes, and one committed 27 crimes.

- Duke has committed more crimes than Lena, but *fewer* crimes than Archie.

- Jo has committed *four* more crimes than Archie.

Can you figure out how many crimes each criminal claims to have committed?

38. Moriarty's Dilemma

The informer who works for Holmes has asked to meet with him. He is terrified because he knows that Moriarty has worked out that someone in his group is leaking information to Holmes.

Moriarty has told the potential suspects in his gang that he will work out who the informer is by giving each of them a test. He has told them this:

> "You must tell me something of your own choice. If what you say is true, I will accept that you are not the informer but I will hold you in my prison for a month in order to be sure. If what you tell me is false, however, then I will know that you are the informer."

The informer has asked Holmes what he should say. He does not wish to be held in Moriarty's prison, but nor does he wish to be revealed as the informer.

What does Holmes advise? What can the man say so that Moriarty will be forced to find a third option?

ANSWERS

1. THE CODED TIP

The message reads, "The robbery will be at noon tomorrow."

2. SCIENCE SUSPECTS

If you rewrite the note using the chemical element abbreviations shown on the poster on the wall, it reads, "It was TiNa!" So the kidnapper was Tina.

3. THE ANONYMOUS LETTER

The note says, "Be careful! There will be a robbery at your gallery!"

4. THE DIAMOND BOX

542

5. MISSING KEYS

1 – B   2 – C   3 – A   4 – D

6. MORIARTY'S WAREHOUSE

Moriarty is using house number 2.

7. A QUESTION OF ROOMS

The auditorium

8. HOLMES'S DIARY

Year = 52 (add 3, 6, 9, 12, 15)
Month = 6 (divide by 2 at each step)
Day = 16 (subtract 1, 3, 5, 7, 9)
His birthdate is therefore the 16th of June '52.

9. A NOTE FROM HOLMES

Solving the equations reveals that:

Therefore Watson should meet him at 368 Edgware Road.

10. THE CALENDAR DEDUCTION

It took place on the 21st of September.

11. IDENTITY PARADE

From left to right as pictured: Sebastian, Jim, Arthur, Thomas and Robert.

12. A CRIMINAL PURSUIT

13. A NOTE FOR WATSON

Thursday

14. HOLMES'S DOMINOES

1 – I   2 – G   3 – H   4 – B
5 – C   6 – E   7 – D

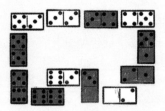

15. MRS HUDSON'S HERBS

16. TRAVEL TIME

30 minutes (walk to station) + 60 minutes (train journey) + 15 minutes (walk to village) = 105 minutes = 1 hour and 45 minutes

17. THE CASE FILES

He solved 81 cases: 8 in January, 2 in February, 3 in March, 4 in April, 3 in May, 8 in each of June and July, and 9 in each of August, September, October, November and December.

18. MORIARTY'S MAP

E: Tower of London

19. THE INNKEEPER'S SECRET

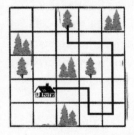

20. THE SECOND ANONYMOUS LETTER

The note says, "A warning! Do not trust your staff! It is one of them!"

21. A CONFUSING TIME

4pm. The time that is "as many hours after 7am as it was before 7pm" is 1pm, since it is 6 hours after 7am and 6 hours before 7pm. Therefore the time "3 hours after" must be 4pm.

22. THE BURGLARY ROUTE

They are planning to burgle houses B, D, E and F. Following the route backwards gives:

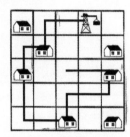

23. THE COFFEE HOUSE SUSPECTS

Suspect 1 arrived at 11am. Suspect 2 arrived at 3 pm. Suspect 3 arrived at 10am. Suspect 4 arrived at 1pm. This means that suspect 4 is the most likely criminal, since they were the only one there at 1:15pm when the crime took place.

24. LIBRARY LOGIC

Nine.

25. A CHRISTMAS CONUNDRUM

Jean is 6 and enjoys painting. Arthur is 7 and plays the guitar. Mary is 9 and likes reading. Lucas is 10 and likes swimming.

26. A MYSTERY PARTY

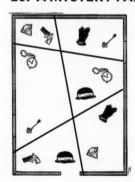

27. THE HIDDEN SUSPECT

He is hiding in the house in D5.

28. THE JEWEL POUCH

Three

29. THE NARROW DOORWAY

Watson was first, followed by Mark, Ruth, Nina and then finally Holmes.

30. THE NUMBER CLUES

By solving the two puzzles, Watson discovered that the correct apartment number was 62:

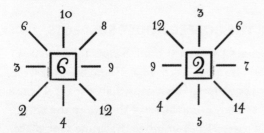

31. ON THE HUNT

They find four eggs along the route, and they end up at the basket of Easter eggs:

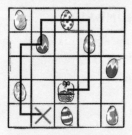

32. A PAINTING PROBLEM

The number of paintings stolen is equal to the number of letters in the artist's name. This means that the thieves stole six Titian paintings.

33. THE ALIBI ARREST

The second suspect. That evening it was raining heavily, so he was very unlikely to be having a picnic in the park.

34. A TEST OF TIME

He should set the watch to 4pm. At this time of day there will have already been 16 hours passed since midnight, and there are 8 hours left until the next midnight at the end of the day.

35. THE DANCING DUOS

Mrs Jones partnered with Mr Jake; Holmes partnered with Ms White; Watson partnered with Mrs Reece; Mrs Hudson partnered with Mr Bradley.

36. A QUICK WAY HOME

The train to Paddington will get them home in 1 hour and 30 minutes. The train to Victoria will get them home in 1 hour and 35 minutes. The train to Liverpool Street will get them home in 1 hour and 40 minutes. Therefore they should take the first train.

37. THE FOUR CRIMINALS

Jo has committed 27 crimes. Lena has committed 16 crimes. Archie has committed 23 crimes. Duke has committed 19 crimes.

38. MORIARTY'S DILEMMA

The informer should tell Moriarty, "I am the informer!". If Moriarty thinks this is true, then by virtue of this being a true statement, Moriarty has to accept that he is not the informer. But if Moriarty believes that the gang member is lying, by virtue of the words of his second statement, then he has to believe that the gang member is actually the informer! In either case, neither of Moriarty's statements to find the truth make sense. So, to actually find the truth, he will have to come up with a third option.